Apples

Publications International, Ltd.

Pictured on the front cover: Tiny Taffy Apples *(page 28)*.
Pictured on the back cover *(counterclockwise from top right)*: Apple Pie Pops *(page 42)*, Sausage & Apple Quiche *(page 12)*, Sun-Dried Tomato, Chicken Sausage, Fennel and Apple Flatbread *(page 52)* and Caramel Apple Cupcakes *(page 32)*.

ISBN: 978-1-68022-759-8

Library of Congress Control Number: 2016958003

Manufactured in China.

8 7 6 5 4 3 2 1

Microwave Cooking: Microwave ovens vary in wattage. Use the cooking times as guidelines and check for doneness before adding more time.

Contents

Cinnamon Chip Applesauce Coffee Cake

MAKES 12 TO 15 SERVINGS

1 cup (2 sticks) butter or margarine, softened	1 teaspoon baking soda
1 cup granulated sugar	½ teaspoon salt
2 eggs	1⅔ cups (10-ounce package) HERSHEY'S® Cinnamon Chips
½ teaspoon vanilla extract	1 cup chopped pecans (optional)
¾ cup applesauce	¾ cup powdered sugar
2½ cups all-purpose flour	1 to 2 tablespoons warm water

1. Heat oven to 350°F. Lightly grease 13×9×2-inch baking pan.

2. Beat butter and granulated sugar with electric mixer on medium speed in large bowl until well blended. Beat in eggs and vanilla. Mix in applesauce. Stir together flour, baking soda and salt; gradually add to butter mixture, beating until well blended. Stir in cinnamon chips and pecans, if desired. Spread in prepared pan.

3. Bake 30 to 35 minutes or until wooden pick inserted in center comes out clean. Cool in pan on wire rack. Sprinkle cake with powdered sugar or stir together ¾ cup powdered sugar and warm water to make smooth glaze; drizzle over cake. Serve at room temperature or while still slightly warm.

FLUTED CAKE: Grease and flour 12-cup fluted tube pan. Prepare batter as directed; pour into prepared pan. Bake 45 to 50 minutes or until wooden pick inserted in thickest part comes out clean. Cool 15 minutes; invert onto wire rack. Cool completely.

CUPCAKES: Line 24 baking cups (2½ inches in diameter) with paper bake cups. Prepare batter as directed; divide evenly into prepared cups. Bake 15 to 18 minutes or until wooden pick inserted in center comes out clean. Cool completely.

Breakfast & Brunch

Oatmeal with Apples and Cottage Cheese

MAKES 2 SERVINGS

½ **cup uncooked oats**

½ **cup diced apple**

⅔ **cup water**

½ **cup cottage cheese**

¾ **teaspoon ground cinnamon**

1 **teaspoon vanilla**

Dash salt

¼ **cup half-and-half**

2 **tablespoons chopped pecans**

1½ **tablespoons sugar**

Combine oats, apple, water, cottage cheese, cinnamon, vanilla and salt in large microwave-safe bowl; stir to blend. Cover with wet paper towel and microwave on HIGH 2 minutes. Let stand 2 minutes. Add half-and-half, pecans and sugar; stir to blend. Serve.

Apple Tea Latte

MAKES 1 SERVING

1   **cup nonfat soy milk**

1   **teaspoon honey**

½   **medium apple, chopped**

1   **LIPTON® Black Pearl Black Pyramid Tea Bag**

1. In 1-quart saucepan, bring soy milk, honey and apple to a boil over high heat. Reduce heat to low and simmer, stirring frequently, 3 minutes.

2. Remove saucepan from heat and add LIPTON® Black Pearl Black Pyramid Tea Bag and brew 3 minutes. Remove tea bag and squeeze. Strain into mug.

Apple Fritters with Two Sauces

MAKES 4 SERVINGS

APPLE FRITTERS

Peanut oil or vegetable oil for deep frying

- 1 cup whole milk
- ¼ cup (½ stick) unsalted butter, melted

  Freshly grated peel and juice of 1 large orange
- 1 egg
- 1 teaspoon vanilla
- 1 large tart apple, peeled, cored and chopped
- 3 cups sifted all-purpose flour
- ½ cup granulated sugar
- 1 tablespoon baking powder
- ½ teaspoon salt

  Powdered sugar

STRAWBERRY SAUCE

- 1 package (12 ounces) frozen unsweetened strawberries, thawed

BUTTERSCOTCH SAUCE

- 6 tablespoons unsalted butter
- ¼ cup granulated sugar
- ¼ cup packed dark brown sugar
- ⅔ cup whipping cream
- 1½ tablespoons lemon juice
- 1 teaspoon vanilla

1. For fritters, heat 2 to 2½ inches oil in heavy saucepan over medium-high heat until 350°F on deep-fry thermometer; adjust heat to maintain temperature.

2. Combine milk, butter, orange peel and juice, egg and vanilla in large bowl; beat until well blended. Stir in apple. Combine flour, granulated sugar, baking powder and salt in medium bowl; gradually stir into milk mixture until blended. (Batter will be thick.)

3. Drop batter by ¼ cupfuls into hot oil. Fry 3 to 4 fritters at a time 8 to 10 minutes, turning often, until evenly browned and crisp. Drain on paper towels.

4. For strawberry sauce, process strawberries in blender until smooth.

5. For butterscotch sauce, melt butter in small saucepan over medium-high heat. Add sugars; stir until melted. Stir in cream; simmer 2 minutes. Remove from heat; stir in lemon juice and vanilla.

6. Place fritters on serving platter; dust with powdered sugar. Serve with strawberry and butterscotch sauces for dipping.

Apple-Raspberry Granola Skillet

MAKES 8 SERVINGS

1 cup granola without raisins

2 tablespoons water

1 tablespoon lemon juice

2 teaspoons cornstarch

1 pound apples, cored and sliced

½ teaspoon ground cinnamon

4 ounces frozen unsweetened raspberries

1 tablespoon sugar

½ teaspoon vanilla

¼ teaspoon almond extract

1. Place granola in small resealable food storage bag; seal tightly. Crush to coarse crumb texture; set aside.

2. Combine water, lemon juice and cornstarch in small bowl; stir until cornstarch is completely dissolved.

3. Combine apples, cornstarch mixture and cinnamon in large skillet; stir until blended. Heat over medium-high heat. Bring to a boil. Boil 1 minute or until thickened, stirring constantly.

4. Remove skillet from heat. Gently fold in raspberries, sugar, vanilla and almond extract. Sprinkle granola crumbs evenly over top. Let stand, uncovered, 30 minutes.

Apple Cinnamon Grill

MAKES 4 SERVINGS

4   teaspoons vegetable-oil-and-yogurt spread

8   slices whole grain cinnamon raisin bread

¼   cup cream cheese

1   medium Granny Smith apple (about 5 ounces), thinly sliced

¼   cup red raspberry preserves

⅛   teaspoon ground cinnamon

1. Spread ½ teaspoon spread onto one side of bread slices. Spread 1 tablespoon cream cheese on opposite side of four bread slices. Arrange apple slices over cream cheese. Spread 1 tablespoon preserves on opposite side of remaining four bread slices; sprinkle with cinnamon. Place on top of apples to create sandwich.

2. Spray large nonstick skillet with nonstick cooking spray; heat over medium heat. Grill sandwiches 2 to 3 minutes on each side or until golden brown.

Sausage & Apple Quiche

MAKES 6 SERVINGS

1 unbaked deep-dish 9-inch pie crust

½ pound bulk spicy pork sausage

½ cup chopped onion

¾ cup shredded peeled tart apple

1 tablespoon lemon juice

1 tablespoon sugar

⅛ teaspoon red pepper flakes

1 cup (4 ounces) shredded Cheddar cheese

1½ cups half-and-half

3 eggs

¼ teaspoon salt

Dash black pepper

1. Preheat oven to 450°F. Line crust with foil; partially fill with uncooked beans or rice. Bake 10 minutes. Remove foil and beans; bake crust 5 minutes or until lightly browned. Let cool. *Reduce oven temperature to 375°F.*

2. Crumble sausage into large skillet; add onion. Cook and stir over medium heat until sausage is browned and onion is tender. Spoon off and discard pan drippings. Add apple, lemon juice, sugar and red pepper flakes; cook and stir 4 minutes or until apple is barely tender and all liquid is evaporated. Let cool. Spoon sausage mixture into crust; sprinkle with cheese.

3. Whisk half-and-half, eggs, salt and black pepper in medium bowl. Pour over sausage mixture in crust.

4. Bake 35 to 45 minutes or until filling is puffed and knife inserted in center comes out clean. Let stand 10 minutes before serving.

Apple Berry Cinnamon Roll Skillet Cobbler

MAKES 8 SERVINGS

- 1 tablespoon cornstarch
- 2 tablespoons lemon juice
- 5 apples (about 2 pounds), peeled and cut into ½-inch pieces
- ½ cup packed brown sugar
- ¾ teaspoon ground cinnamon
- ⅛ teaspoon ground ginger
- 3 tablespoons butter
- ½ cup coarsely chopped pecans
- 1 cup fresh blueberries
- 1 package (13 ounces) refrigerated flaky cinnamon rolls with icing

1. Preheat oven to 350°F.

2. Stir cornstarch into lemon juice in small bowl until blended. Combine apples, brown sugar, cinnamon and ginger in large bowl; mix well. Add cornstarch mixture; toss to coat.

3. Melt butter in large (12-inch) cast iron skillet over medium heat. Add apple mixture and pecans; press into single layer to cover bottom of skillet. Sprinkle with blueberries.

4. Bake 20 minutes. Remove skillet from oven. Separate cinnamon rolls; reserve icing. Arrange cinnamon rolls over warm fruit mixture.

5. Bake 20 to 25 minutes or until filling is bubbly and cinnamon rolls are deep golden brown. Drizzle with icing. Let stand 5 minutes before serving.

Apple-Cheddar Muffins

MAKES 12 MUFFINS

1 cup whole wheat flour

1 cup all-purpose white flour

2 tablespoons sugar

1 tablespoon baking powder

½ teaspoon salt

1 cup peeled, chopped apple

1 cup grated **CABOT® Mild or Sharp Cheddar**

2 large eggs

1 cup milk

4 tablespoons **CABOT® Salted Butter, melted**

1. Preheat oven to 400°F. Butter 12 muffin cups or coat with nonstick cooking spray.

2. In mixing bowl, stir together whole wheat and white flours, sugar, baking powder and salt. Add apples and cheese; toss to combine.

3. In another bowl, whisk eggs lightly. Whisk in milk and butter. Make well in center of dry ingredients; add milk mixture and gently stir in dry ingredients from side until just combined.

4. Divide batter among prepared muffin cups. Bake 20 minutes, or until muffins feel firm when lightly pressed on top.

German Apple Pancake

MAKES 6 SERVINGS

1 tablespoon butter

1 large *or* 2 small apples, peeled and thinly sliced (about 1½ cups)

1 tablespoon packed brown sugar

1½ teaspoons ground cinnamon, divided

2 eggs

2 egg whites

1 tablespoon granulated sugar

1 teaspoon vanilla

¼ teaspoon salt

½ cup all-purpose flour

½ cup milk

Maple syrup (optional)

1. Preheat oven to 425°F.

2. Melt butter in medium cast iron or ovenproof skillet* over medium heat. Add apples, brown sugar and ½ teaspoon cinnamon; cook and stir 5 minutes or until apples just begin to soften. Remove from heat. Arrange apple slices in single layer in skillet.

3. Whisk eggs, egg whites, granulated sugar, remaining 1 teaspoon cinnamon, vanilla and salt in medium bowl until well blended. Stir in flour and milk until smooth and well blended. Pour evenly over apples.

4. Bake 20 to 25 minutes or until puffed and golden brown. Serve with syrup, if desired.

To make skillet ovenproof, wrap handle in foil.

Note: Pancake will fall slightly after being removed from the oven.

Oatmeal Waffles with Spiced Apple Compote

MAKES 6 SERVINGS

APPLE COMPOTE

- **2 tablespoons unsalted butter**
- **1 pound Granny Smith apples, peeled, cored and cut into ½-inch pieces**
- **¼ cup maple syrup**
- **½ cup water**
- **¼ cup raisins**
- **1 teaspoon ground cinnamon**

WAFFLES

- **1¼ cups quick-cooking oats**
- **¾ cup oat flour**
- **¼ cup flax meal**
- **½ teaspoon salt**
- **1 tablespoon baking powder**
- **1¾ cups hot milk**
- **8 tablespoons (1 stick) unsalted butter, melted and slightly cooled**
- **3 eggs**
- **¼ cup maple syrup**

1. Preheat Belgium waffle maker to medium-high heat. Set wire rack on top of large baking sheet.

2. Prepare apple compote. Melt 2 tablespoons butter in large nonstick skillet over medium-high heat. Add apples, ¼ cup syrup, water, raisins and cinnamon; stir to combine. Reduce heat to medium, cover and cook 5 minutes. Uncover; continue cooking 5 minutes or until apples are tender and most of liquid has evaporated, stirring occasionally. Set aside.

3. Prepare waffles. Combine oats, flour, flax meal, salt and baking powder in large bowl. Pour in hot milk; stir until combined. Let stand 5 minutes.

4. Combine 8 tablespoons melted butter, eggs and ¼ cup syrup in large bowl. Pour into oat mixture; stir until combined.

5. Pour ⅓ cup batter into each well of waffle maker. Close lid; cook 6 minutes or until golden brown. Remove waffles to wire rack in oven; tent with foil to keep warm. Repeat with remaining batter.

6. Serve waffles with apple compote.

Apple-Cheddar Scones

MAKES 8 SCONES

1¾ cups all-purpose flour

¾ cup plus 2 tablespoons buttermilk

1 tablespoon sugar

1 teaspoon baking powder

¾ teaspoon dried thyme

¼ teaspoon baking soda

¼ teaspoon salt

6 tablespoons cold butter, cut into small pieces

1 apple, peeled, cored and chopped

½ cup plus 2 tablespoons shredded Cheddar cheese, divided

½ cup water

1. Preheat oven to 400°F. Lightly grease large baking sheet.

2. Combine flour, buttermilk, sugar, baking powder, thyme, baking soda and salt in large bowl; stir to blend. Cut in butter with pastry blender until mixture resembles coarse crumbs. Stir in apple and ½ cup cheese. Stir in water until soft dough forms; form into a ball.

3. Place dough on prepared baking sheet. Press into 8-inch round with lightly floured hands. Cut into eight wedges with lightly floured knife; slightly separate pieces by moving knife back and forth between slices. Sprinkle remaining 2 tablespoons cheese evenly over wedges.

4. Bake 20 minutes or until lightly browned. Remove scones to wire rack; cool completely. Store in airtight container at room temperature up to 3 days.

Cider-Poached Apples with Cinnamon Yogurt

MAKES 4 SERVINGS

2 cups apple cider or apple juice

1 cinnamon stick *or* ½ teaspoon ground cinnamon

2 Golden Delicious apples, peeled, halved and cored

½ cup vanilla yogurt

½ teaspoon ground cinnamon

½ cup chopped pecans, toasted

1. Bring apple cider and cinnamon stick to a boil in medium saucepan over high heat. Boil, uncovered, 25 minutes or until liquid is reduced to about 1 cup.

2. Add apples; cover and simmer 10 minutes or until apples are just tender. Gently remove apples; discard poaching liquid. Refrigerate until completely cool.

3. Combine yogurt and ground cinnamon in small bowl; reserve 2 tablespoons. Divide remaining yogurt mixture evenly among four dessert dishes. Place apple halves on top of sauce. Sprinkle each apple half with 2 tablespoons toasted pecans. Drizzle with reserved yogurt sauce.

Tip: To toast the pecans, spread in a single layer on a baking sheet and toast in a preheated 350°F oven 8 to 10 minutes or until very lightly browned. Use immediately or store in a covered container in the refrigerator.

Apple Date Nut Muffins

MAKES 12 MUFFINS

1½ **cups all-purpose flour**

⅔ **cup packed brown sugar**

½ **cup old-fashioned oats**

1 **tablespoon baking powder**

1 **teaspoon ground cinnamon**

½ **teaspoon salt**

⅛ **teaspoon ground nutmeg**

⅛ **teaspoon ground ginger**

Dash ground cloves

1 **cup coarsely chopped peeled apples**

½ **cup chopped walnuts**

½ **cup chopped pitted dates**

½ **cup (1 stick) butter, melted**

2 **eggs**

¼ **cup milk**

1. Preheat oven to 400°F. Line 12 standard (2½-inch) muffin cups with paper baking cups or spray with nonstick cooking spray.

2. Combine flour, brown sugar, oats, baking powder, cinnamon, salt, nutmeg, ginger and cloves in large bowl. Mix in apples, walnuts and dates.

3. Whisk butter, eggs and milk in small bowl until blended. Stir into flour mixture just until moistened. Spoon batter evenly into prepared muffin cups.

4. Bake 20 to 25 minutes or until toothpick inserted into centers comes out clean. Remove to wire rack; cool completely.

Tiny Taffy Apples

MAKES ABOUT 24 POPS

4 medium apples, peeled and chopped (about 4 cups)

Juice of ½ lemon

1 cup plus 1 tablespoon sugar, divided

3 cups all-purpose flour

1½ teaspoons baking soda

1 teaspoon ground cinnamon

½ teaspoon salt

½ teaspoon ground nutmeg

1 cup vegetable oil

1 teaspoon vanilla

½ cup plus 2 tablespoons frosting

1 package (14 to 16 ounces) peanut butter candy coating

24 lollipop sticks

2 cups chopped peanuts

24 paper baking cups (optional)

1. Preheat oven to 350°F. Spray 13X9-inch baking pan with nonstick cooking spray. Place apples in medium bowl. Drizzle with lemon juice and sprinkle with 1 tablespoon sugar; toss to coat. Let stand 20 minutes or until juice forms.

2. Combine flour, remaining 1 cup sugar, baking soda, cinnamon, salt and nutmeg in large bowl; mix well. Add oil and vanilla; stir until well blended. Stir in apple mixture. Spread batter in prepared pan.

3. Bake 35 minutes or until browned and tootpick inserted into center comes out clean. Cool completely in pan on wire rack.

4. Line large baking sheet with waxed paper. Use hands to crumble half of cake into large bowl. (You should end up with fine crumbs and no large cake pieces remaining.) Reserve remaining half of cake for another use.

5. Add frosting to cake crumbs; mix with hands until well blended. Shape mixture into 1½-inch balls (about 2 tablespoons cake mixture per ball); place on prepared baking sheet. Cover with plastic wrap; refrigerate at least 1 hour or freeze 10 minutes to firm.

6. When cake balls are firm, place candy coating in large deep microwavable bowl. Melt according to package directions. Dip one lollipop stick about ½ inch into melted coating; insert stick into cake ball (no more than halfway through). Return cake pop to baking sheet in refrigerator to set. Repeat with remaining cake balls and sticks.

7. Place peanuts in shallow bowl. Working with one cake pop at a time, hold stick and dip cake ball into melted coating to cover completely, letting excess coating drip off. Rotate stick gently and/or tap stick on edge of bowl, if necessary, to remove excess coating.

8. Immediately roll cake pop in peanuts to coat; press peanuts in gently to adhere to coating. Place cake pops in baking cups, if desired.

Apple Treats

Apple Granola Pizza with Vanilla Drizzle

MAKES 1 (12-INCH) PIZZA

PIZZA

1¾ to 2¼ cups all-purpose flour, divided

1 envelope FLEISCHMANN'S® Pizza Crust Yeast or RapidRise Yeast

2 tablespoons granulated sugar

¾ teaspoon salt

⅔ cup very warm water (120° to 130°F)

3 tablespoons melted butter or margarine

1 can (21 ounces) apple pie filling

⅔ cup granola cereal

VANILLA DRIZZLE

1 cup powdered sugar

½ teaspoon SPICE ISLANDS® 100% Pure Bourbon Vanilla Extract

1 to 2 tablespoons milk

COMBINE 1 cup flour, undissolved yeast, granulated sugar and salt in a large bowl. Add very warm water and butter; mix until well blended, about 1 minute. Gradually add enough remaining flour to make a soft dough. Dough should form a ball and will be slightly sticky.

KNEAD on a floured surface, adding additional flour if necessary, until smooth and elastic, about 4 minutes. (If using RapidRise yeast, let dough rest at this point for 10 minutes). Pat dough with floured hands, pressing gently to fill greased pizza pan or baking sheet, or roll dough on a floured counter to 12-inch circle; place in greased pizza pan or baking sheet. Form a rim by pinching the edge of the dough.

SPREAD apple pie filling over crust; top with granola cereal.

BAKE in a preheated 450°F oven on lowest oven rack for 12 to 15 minutes, until crust is browned and granola topping is lightly browned. Remove from oven and cool 5 minutes. Combine Vanilla Drizzle ingredients in a small bowl. Drizzle over pizza.

SERVE warm.

Caramel Apple Cupcakes

MAKES 24 CUPCAKES

1 package (about 15 ounces) butter recipe yellow cake mix, plus ingredients to prepare mix

1 cup chopped dried apples

Caramel Frosting (recipe follows)

Chopped pecans (optional)

1. Preheat oven to 375°F. Line 24 standard (2½-inch) muffin cups with paper baking cups.

2. Prepare cake mix according to package directions; stir in apples. Spoon batter into prepared muffin cups, filling two-thirds full.

3. Bake 20 minutes or until toothpick inserted into centers comes out clean. Cool in pans 10 minutes. Remove to wire racks; cool completely.

4. Prepare Caramel Frosting. Frost cupcakes; sprinkle with pecans, if desired.

Caramel Frosting

MAKES ABOUT 3 CUPS

3 tablespoons butter

1 cup packed light brown sugar

½ cup evaporated milk

⅛ teaspoon salt

3¾ cups powdered sugar

¾ teaspoon vanilla

1. Melt butter in medium saucepan. Stir in brown sugar, evaporated milk and salt. Bring to a boil, stirring constantly. Remove from heat to large bowl; cool slightly.

2. Add powdered sugar; beat with electric mixer at medium speed until smooth. Add vanilla; beat until smooth and frosting reaches desired spreading consistency.

Sautéed Apples Supreme

MAKES 2 SERVINGS

2 **small apples *or* 1 large apple**

1 **teaspoon butter**

¼ **cup unsweetened apple juice or cider**

2 **teaspoons packed brown sugar**

½ **teaspoon ground cinnamon**

⅔ **cup vanilla ice cream or frozen yogurt (optional)**

1 **tablespoon chopped walnuts, toasted***

*To toast walnuts, spread in single layer in heavy-bottomed skillet. Cook over medium heat 1 to 2 minutes, stirring frequently until lightly browned. Remove from skillet immediately. Cool before using.

1. Cut apples into quarters; remove cores and cut into ½-inch-thick slices.

2. Melt butter in large nonstick skillet over medium heat. Add apples; cook 4 minutes, stirring occasionally.

3. Combine apple juice, brown sugar and cinnamon in small bowl; pour over apples. Simmer 5 minutes or until apples are tender and sauce thickens. Transfer to serving bowls; serve with ice cream, if desired. Sprinkle with walnuts.

Apple-Walnut Glazed Spice Baby Cakes

MAKES 12 CAKES

- **1 package (about 15 ounces) spice cake mix**
- **1⅓ cups plus 3 tablespoons water, divided**
- **3 eggs**
- **⅓ cup vegetable oil**
- **½ teaspoon vanilla, butter and nut flavoring***
- **¾ cup chopped walnuts**

- **12 ounces Granny Smith apples, peeled and cut into ½-inch cubes (about 3 medium)**
- **¼ teaspoon ground cinnamon**
- **1 jar (12 ounces) caramel ice cream topping**

Vanilla, butter and nut flavoring is available in the baking aisles of most large supermarkets.

1. Preheat oven to 350°F. Grease and flour 12 small (1-cup) bundt pan cups.

2. Beat cake mix, 1⅓ cups water, eggs, oil and flavoring in large bowl 30 seconds with electric mixer at low speed. Beat at medium speed 2 minutes. Spoon batter evenly into prepared bundt cups.

3. Bake 25 minutes or until toothpick inserted near centers comes out clean. Cool in pans 15 minutes. Remove to wire racks; cool completely.

4. Meanwhile, place large skillet over medium heat. Add walnuts; cook and stir 3 minutes or until lightly browned. Transfer to small bowl. Add apples, remaining 3 tablespoons water and cinnamon to skillet; cook and stir 3 minutes or until apples are crisp-tender. Remove from heat; stir in walnuts and caramel topping. Spoon apple mixture over cakes.

Candy Bar Taffy Apple Salad

MAKES ABOUT 8 CUPS

2   **apples, chopped**

2   **cups miniature marshmallows**

2   **cups thawed frozen whipped topping**

1   **cup chopped chocolate candy bars**

½   **cup salted peanuts**

Combine apples, marshmallows, whipped topping, candy bars and peanuts in large bowl; stir to blend. Refrigerate 1 hour before serving.

Tip: The peak season for domestically grown apples, when flavor and texture are at their best, is September through November. Apples imported from Australia and New Zealand, such as Braeburn, Granny Smith, Gala and Royal Gala, are at their peak from April through July. Since these varieties are also grown in the United States, check labels or ask the produce manager to ensure that spring and summer apples have been imported from the Southern Hemisphere.

Grilled Apples with Brown Sugar and Cinnamon

MAKES 4 SERVINGS

2 tablespoons packed brown sugar

1 tablespoon ground cinnamon

¼ teaspoon ground nutmeg

2 large apples (Red Delicious, Braeburn or Fuji), cored and sliced into 12 rings

Caramel or butterscotch sauce

Vanilla ice cream (optional)

1. Combine brown sugar, cinnamon and nutmeg in small bowl. Sprinkle onto apple slices.

2. Wrap apples in foil. Place on grill over medium-low heat. Cook until tender, turning as needed, until rich brown, but not mushy, about 9 minutes.

3. Place on four plates and drizzle with warmed caramel sauce. Add ice cream, if desired.

Note: A variety of fruit works great on the grill. Also try peaches wrapped in foil, sprinkled with brown sugar, cinnamon and butter. Grill 8 to 12 minutes until the fruit becomes soft.

Apple Monte Cristos

MAKES 2 SANDWICHES

4 ounces Gouda cheese, shredded	1 small apple, cored and thinly sliced
1 ounce cream cheese, softened	¼ cup milk
2 teaspoons honey	1 egg, beaten
½ teaspoon ground cinnamon	1 tablespoon butter
4 slices cinnamon raisin bread	Powdered sugar

1. Combine Gouda cheese, cream cheese, honey and cinnamon in small bowl; stir until well blended. Spread cheese mixture evenly on all bread slices. Layer apple slices evenly over cheese on 2 bread slices; top with remaining bread slices.

2. Combine milk and egg in shallow bowl; stir until well blended. Dip sandwiches in egg mixture, turning to coat well.

3. Melt butter in large nonstick skillet over medium heat. Add sandwiches; cook 4 to 5 minutes per side or until cheese melts and sandwiches are golden brown. Sprinkle with powdered sugar.

Apple Pie Pops

MAKES 4 POPS

1 refrigerated pie crust (½ of 15-ounce package)

1½ teaspoons packed brown sugar

1 tablespoon milk

4 (5-ounce) paper or plastic cups

1¼ cups vanilla ice cream

1 cup apple pie filling

1 teaspoon pumpkin pie spice

4 pop sticks

1. Preheat oven to 450°F. Line large baking sheet with parchment paper. Let pie crust stand at room temperature 15 minutes.

2. Roll pie crust onto prepared baking sheet. Prick with fork. Bake 10 to 12 minutes or until golden brown. Cool completely on baking sheet.

3. Crumble pie crust. Combine ½ cup crumbs and brown sugar in small bowl; mix well. Discard remaining crumbs or save for future use. Add milk to crumb mixture, mixing and mashing with fork until well blended. Press about 2 tablespoons crumb mixture into each cup, using wet fingers if necessary.

4. Combine ice cream, pie filling and pumpkin pie spice in blender or food processor; blend until smooth.

5. Pour ice cream mixture into cups over crumb base. Cover top of each cup with small piece of foil. Insert sticks through center of foil. Freeze 6 hours or until firm.

6. To serve, remove foil and peel away paper cups or gently twist frozen pops out of plastic cups.

Fudge, Apple and Pecan Tizzies

MAKES 2 SERVINGS

2 tablespoons sugar	**1** apple, cored and cut into 8 wedges
½ teaspoon ground cinnamon	**2** tablespoons hot fudge topping
½ teaspoon cocoa powder	**8** pecan halves, broken in half again

1. Combine sugar, cinnamon and cocoa in small bowl; stir to blend.

2. Place apple wedges on plate; sprinkle with cocoa mixture. Turn apple slices over and sprinkle other side.

3. Spread each apple wedge with 1 teaspoon hot fudge topping. Top with 2 pecan halves. Refrigerate at least 20 minutes before serving.

Cherry and Coke® Apple Rings

MAKES 4 SERVINGS

3 **Granny Smith or other tart apples,
   peeled and cored**

½ **teaspoon plus ¼ teaspoon cherry-
   flavored gelatin powder**

⅓ **cup COCA-COLA®**

⅓ **cup nondairy whipped topping**

Slice apples crosswise into ¼-inch-thick rings; remove seeds. Place stacks of apple rings in large microwavable bowl; sprinkle with gelatin. Pour **COCA-COLA®** over rings.

Cover loosely with waxed paper. Microwave on HIGH (100%) 5 minutes or until liquid is boiling. Allow to stand, covered, 5 minutes. Arrange on dessert plates. Serve warm with whipped topping.

Aztec Apple Empanadas

MAKES 18 EMPANADAS

2 tablespoons butter

3 Red or Golden Delicious apples, peeled, cored and diced

2 tablespoons sugar

1 packet (1.25 ounces) ORTEGA® Reduced Sodium Chili Seasoning Mix, divided

½ teaspoon ground cinnamon

1 package (about 1 pound) frozen puff pastry sheets, thawed

1 egg, lightly beaten

PREHEAT oven to 350°F. Lightly grease baking sheet or lightly coat with nonstick cooking spray.

MELT butter in large skillet over medium-high heat. Add apples, sugar, 2 tablespoons seasoning mix and cinnamon; toss to coat apples evenly. Reduce heat; cook about 5 minutes or until apples begin to soften. Remove from heat; set aside.

UNFOLD puff pastry sheets on lightly floured surface. Cut each puff pastry sheet into 9 squares.

PLACE scant tablespoon apple mixture into center of each pastry square. Fold pastry over filling to form triangles. Press edges with fork to seal. Place on prepared baking sheet. Brush top of each pastry with egg.

BAKE 15 minutes or until just beginning to brown. Remove from oven; cool 5 minutes on wire rack. Sprinkle remaining seasoning mix evenly onto empanadas. Serve warm or at room temperature.

Caramel Apple Nachos

MAKES 8 SERVINGS

10 caramels, unwrapped

2 tablespoons half-and-half

2 apples, thinly sliced

¼ cup mini chocolate chips

½ cup candy-coated chocolate pieces

1. Combine caramels and half-and-half in small saucepan over low heat; cook and stir just until melted.

2. Layer apple slices on large platter; drizzle with caramel sauce. Sprinkle with chocolate chips and candy pieces.

Tip: Choose apples that are firm, fragrant and a bright color. The skin should be tight without bruises, blemishes or punctures. An apple should not yield when squeezed or pinched. Brown streaks, called russeting or scalds, on the skin are present in some varieties but won't affect quality.

Apple-Pecan Cheesecake

MAKES ONE 9-INCH CHEESECAKE

2　packages (8 ounces each) cream cheese, softened

⅔　cup sugar, divided

2　eggs

½　teaspoon vanilla

1　(9-inch) prepared graham cracker crust

½　teaspoon ground cinnamon

4　cups Golden Delicious apples, peeled, cored and thinly sliced (about 2½ pounds apples)

½　cup chopped pecans

1. Preheat oven to 350°F.

2. Beat cream cheese and ⅓ cup sugar in large bowl with electric mixer at medium speed until well blended. Add eggs, one at a time, beating well after each addition. Blend in vanilla; pour into crust.

3. Combine remaining ⅓ cup sugar and cinnamon in large bowl. Add apples; toss gently to coat. Arrange apple mixture over cream cheese mixture. Sprinkle with pecans.

4. Bake 1 hour and 10 minutes or until set. Cool completely. Store in refrigerator.

Sun-Dried Tomato, Chicken Sausage, Fennel and Apple Flatbread

MAKES 6 SERVINGS

- 2 tablespoons sun-dried tomato dressing
- 1 (10½-ounce) stone-baked pizza crust*
- 1 small red onion, thinly sliced
- ½ fennel bulb, thinly sliced
- 1 fully-cooked sun-dried tomato chicken sausage, thinly sliced
- 1 Granny Smith apple, peeled, cored and thinly sliced
- ¾ cup finely shredded mozzarella cheese
- 2 tablespoons grated Parmesan cheese

*If unavailable, may substitute with a 12-inch prepared pizza crust.

1. Heat oven to 400°F. Spread dressing over crust.

2. Layer onion, fennel, chicken sausage and apple over crust.

3. Sprinkle evenly with cheeses. Bake 20 minutes or until cheeses melt and crust edges are brown.

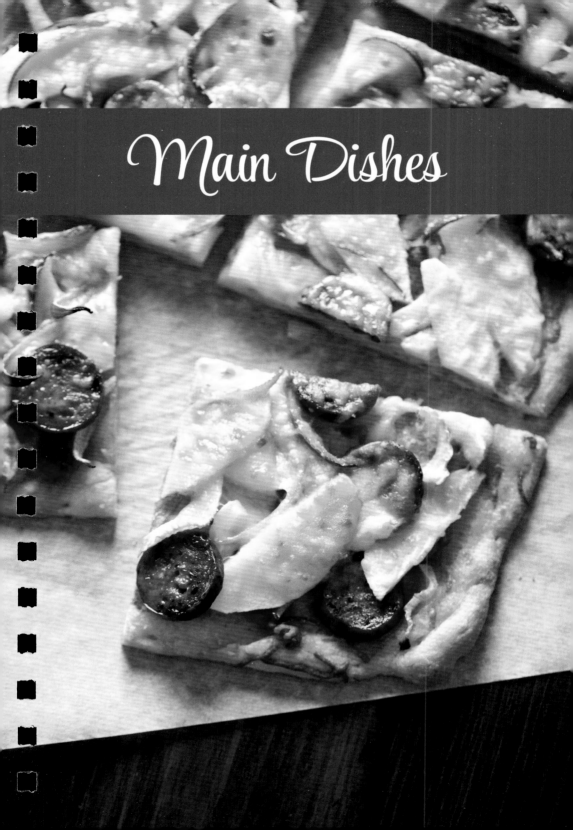

Main Dishes

Mojo Pork with Orange-Apple Salsa

MAKES 6 TO 8 SERVINGS

2 tablespoons olive oil

1 tablespoon minced garlic

½ cup FRANK'S® REDHOT® Original Cayenne Pepper Sauce

½ cup orange juice

2 tablespoons grated orange zest

¼ cup minced fresh cilantro

2 tablespoons chili powder

1 teaspoon dried oregano

2 boneless pork tenderloins (2 pounds)

½ cup sour cream

Orange-Apple Salsa (recipe follows)

HEAT oil over medium heat in small saucepan and cook garlic 2 minutes or until tender. Stir in **FRANK'S® REDHOT®** Original Cayenne Pepper Sauce, orange juice, zest, cilantro, chili powder and oregano. Reserve ¼ *cup* marinade.

PLACE pork in resealable plastic food storage bag or shallow bowl. Pour remaining marinade over pork. Marinate in refrigerator 1 to 3 hours. Combine reserved marinade with sour cream; set aside in refrigerator.

GRILL pork over medium-high direct heat for 20 minutes or until desired doneness. Slice pork and drizzle with spicy sour cream. Serve with Orange-Apple Salsa.

Orange-Apple Salsa

MAKES ABOUT 3 CUPS

3 navel oranges, peeled, sectioned and cut into small pieces

2 large apples, cored and diced

2 tablespoons chopped red onion

2 tablespoons chopped fresh cilantro

2 tablespoons FRANK'S® REDHOT® Original Cayenne Pepper Sauce

Combine ingredients in bowl; chill until ready to serve.

Apple and Turkey Meatballs

MAKES 6 SERVINGS

- **1 pound ground turkey**
- **1½ cups red delicious apple, finely chopped**
- **1 cup shredded hot pepper cheese**
- **½ cup sun-dried tomatoes packed in oil, minced**

- **1 package (12 ounces) spinach linguini pasta**
- **1 jar (18 ounces) HEINZ® HomeStyle Roasted Turkey Gravy**

1. Preheat oven to 400°F. Coat a baking sheet with nonstick cooking spray. In a medium bowl, mix together turkey, apple, cheese and sun-dried tomatoes. Form into 30 meatballs, about 1-inch size. Arrange on baking sheet.

2. Bake uncovered for about 20 minutes, or until internal temperature reaches 165°F.

3. Meanwhile, cook pasta according to package instructions.

4. Meanwhile, in a small saucepan over medium heat, cook gravy for 3 to 5 minutes, or until heated through, stirring occasionally.

5. To serve, divide cooked pasta among each plate and place 5 meatballs on each. Spoon warm gravy on top and serve immediately.

Mu Shu Steak & Apple Wraps

MAKES 4 SERVINGS

4 **beef tri-tip steaks, cut 1-inch thick (about 4 ounces each)**	**Salt (optional)**
¾ **teaspoon ground cinnamon**	3 **cups tri-color coleslaw mix (with green cabbage, red cabbage and carrots)**
¼ **teaspoon pepper**	1 **Granny Smith apple**
¼ **cup hoisin sauce**	8 **medium whole wheat flour tortillas (8- to 10-inch diameter), warmed**
1 **tablespoon honey**	

1. Combine cinnamon and pepper; press evenly onto beef steaks. Heat large nonstick skillet over medium heat. Place steaks in skillet; cook 9 to 12 minutes for medium rare to medium doneness, turning occasionally.

2. Combine hoisin sauce and honey in large bowl. Carve steaks into thin slices; season with salt, if desired. Add steak slices, coleslaw mix and apple to hoisin mixture; toss to coat.

3. Place equal amounts of beef mixture down center of each tortilla, leaving 1½-inch border on right and left sides. Fold bottom edge up over filling. Fold right and left sides to center, overlapping edges; secure with toothpicks, if necessary.

Tip: One boneless beef top sirloin steak, cut ¾-inch thick or 2 beef shoulder center steaks, cut ¾-inch thick (about 1 pound) may be substituted for tri-tip steaks. Pan-broil top sirloin steak 10 to 13 minutes (shoulder center steaks 9 to 12 minutes) for medium rare to medium doneness, turning once.

Courtesy The Beef Checkoff

Pecan and Apple Stuffed Pork Chops with Apple Brandy

MAKES 4 SERVINGS

- **4** **thick-cut, bone-in pork loin chops (about 4 ounces *each*)**
- **1** **teaspoon salt, divided**
- **½** **teaspoon black pepper, divided**
- **2** **tablespoons vegetable oil**
- **½** **cup diced green apple**
- **½** **small onion, minced**
- **¼** **teaspoon dried thyme**
- **½** **cup apple brandy or brandy**
- **⅔** **cup cubed white bread**
- **2** **tablespoons chopped pecans**
- **1** **cup apple juice cocktail**

SLOW COOKER DIRECTIONS

1. Coat inside of slow cooker with nonstick cooking spray. Rinse pork chops and pat dry. Season with ½ teaspoon salt and ¼ teaspoon pepper. Heat oil in large skillet over medium-high heat. Working in batches, brown pork chops about 2 minutes on both sides. Set aside.

2. Add apple, onion, thyme, remaining ½ teaspoon salt and remaining ¼ teaspoon pepper to hot skillet and reduce heat to medium. Cook and stir 3 minutes or until onion is translucent. Remove from heat and pour in brandy. Return to medium heat and simmer until most liquid is absorbed. Stir in bread and pecans; cook 1 minute.

3. Cut each pork chop horizontally with sharp knife to form pocket. Divide stuffing among pork chops. Arrange pork chops in slow cooker, pocket side up.

4. Pour apple juice around pork chops. Cover; cook on HIGH 1½ to 1¾ hours or until pork is 155°F when tested with meat thermometer. (Do not overcook or pork chops will be dry.)

Tip: Consider using your slow cooker as an extra "burner" that doesn't need watching. For example, you can cook this main dish in the slow cooker while you prepare the sides.

Turkey Apple Cranberry Bake

MAKES 4 SERVINGS

1 cup PEPPERIDGE FARM® Herb Seasoned Stuffing

1 tablespoon butter, melted

1 can (10¾ ounces) CAMPBELL'S® Condensed Cream of Celery Soup (Regular *or* 98% Fat Free)

½ cup milk

2 cups cubed cooked turkey

1 medium apple, diced (about 1½ cups)

1 stalk celery, finely chopped (about ½ cup)

½ cup dried cranberries

½ cup pecan halves, chopped

1. Stir the stuffing and butter in a small bowl. Set aside.

2. Stir the soup, milk, turkey, apple, celery, cranberries and pecans in a 12×8×2-inch shallow baking dish. Sprinkle the reserved stuffing mixture over the turkey mixture.

3. Bake at 400°F. for 30 minutes or until hot and bubbly.

Smoked Sausage with Beer-Braised Sauerkraut and Apples

MAKES 4 TO 6 SERVINGS

2 **pounds refrigerated sauerkraut**

1 **tablespoon vegetable oil**

2 **Granny Smith apples, peeled, cored and cut into ½-inch-thick wedges**

1 **medium onion, chopped**

1 **cup lager**

1 **tablespoon packed brown sugar**

1½ **teaspoons caraway seed (optional)**

1½ **pounds smoked sausages, such as chicken-apple**

Black pepper

1. Preheat oven to 325°F.

2. Drain sauerkraut. Rinse under cold water and drain again. Squeeze out excess liquid. Set aside.

3. Heat oil in large ovenproof skillet over medium heat. Add apples; cook and stir 2 minutes or until lightly browned. Add onion; cook and stir 4 minutes or until golden. Stir in sauerkraut, lager, brown sugar and caraway seed, if desired; bring to a boil.

4. Pierce sausages with fork; cover with sauerkraut. Cover skillet, leaving lid slightly ajar. Bake 30 minutes or until sausages are heated through and most beer has evaporated. Season sauerkraut with pepper. Serve immediately.

VARIATION: Use any kind of smoked sausage that you like (kielbasa is also good) or even smoked pork chops.

SERVING SUGGESTION: Serve the smoked sausage with boiled or pan-fried potatoes.

Quinoa, Turkey and Apple Pilaf

MAKES 4 SERVINGS

½ cup uncooked quinoa

1 cup water

1 tablespoon canola oil

1½ cups chopped onions

1 cup chopped red bell pepper

1 cup diced red apple

6 ounces cooked oven-roasted turkey breast, chopped

2 ounces pecan pieces, toasted*

⅓ cup dried apricot halves, chopped

¼ cup chopped fresh cilantro (optional)

1 to 1½ teaspoons grated fresh ginger

1½ teaspoons sugar

½ teaspoon salt

To toast pecans, spread in single layer in heavy skillet. Cook and stir over medium heat 1 to 2 minutes or until nuts are lightly browned.

1. Place quinoa in fine-mesh strainer; rinse well under cold running water. Bring 1 cup water to a boil in small saucepan; stir in quinoa. Reduce heat to low; cover and simmer 15 minutes or until quinoa is tender and water is absorbed. Fluff with fork and set aside to cool.

2. Meanwhile, heat oil in large nonstick skillet over medium-high heat. Cook onions 5 minutes or until beginning to richly brown. Stir in bell pepper and apple; cook 4 minutes or until apple is just crisp-tender. Add turkey and cook 1 minute. Remove from heat, stir in quinoa, pecans, apricots, cilantro, if desired, ginger, sugar and salt. Cover; let stand 5 minutes to absorb flavors.

Apple-Cherry Glazed Pork Chops

MAKES 2 SERVINGS

¼ to ½ teaspoon dried thyme

⅛ teaspoon salt

⅛ teaspoon black pepper

2 boneless pork loin chops (3 ounces each), trimmed of fat

⅔ cup unsweetened apple juice

½ small apple, sliced

2 tablespoons sliced green onion

2 tablespoons dried tart cherries

1 teaspoon cornstarch

1 tablespoon water

1. Combine thyme, salt and pepper in small bowl. Rub onto both sides of pork chops.

2. Spray large skillet with nonstick cooking spray; heat over medium heat. Add pork chops; cook 3 to 5 minutes or until barely pink in center, turning once. Remove to plate; keep warm.

3. Add apple juice, apple slices, green onion and cherries to same skillet. Simmer 2 to 3 minutes or until apple and onion are tender.

4. Stir cornstarch into water in small bowl until smooth; stir into skillet. Bring to a boil; cook and stir until thickened. Spoon apple mixture over pork chops.

Jarlsberg® Apple Slaw Sandwich

- **2 slices Pullman-style white bread**
- **2 slices JARLSBERG® cheese**
- **Extra virgin olive oil**
- **Apple Slaw (recipe follows)**

Apply extra virgin olive oil to one side of each slice of bread. Place both slices, oil side down, on a low-medium heated skillet. Top one bread slice with 2 slices of JARLSBERG® (or about 1½ ounces shredded JARLSBERG®) cheese. Let bread toast and cheese melt before topping cheese with ⅔ cup of Apple Slaw. Cover with the other slice, and continue grilling sandwich on both sides until you have reached "maximum golden toasty-ness."

Apple Slaw
MAKES 6 TO 8 SERVINGS

- **2 teaspoons lemon juice**
- **2 teaspoons honey**
- **2 teaspoons apple cider vinegar**
- **1 tablespoon olive oil**
- **Dash of crushed red pepper flakes**
- **½ large red onion, sliced thin***
- **3 cups of shaved brussels sprouts**
- **1 Gala apple**
- **2 Granny Smith apples**
- **Salt and pepper to taste**
- **You can use a mandolin.*

In large bowl whisk lemon juice, honey, apple cider vinegar, olive oil and crushed red pepper flakes; add sliced onions. Peel outer layer of brussels sprouts, chop off roots, and slice very thin. Core and halve apples, then slice very thin. Add sprouts and apples to bowl, and gently toss until all pieces are coated. Refrigerate 1 hour before serving.

Apple Curry Chicken

MAKES 4 SERVINGS

4 **boneless skinless chicken breasts**	1 **onion, chopped**
1 **cup apple juice, divided**	¼ **cup raisins**
¼ **teaspoon salt**	2 **teaspoons packed brown sugar**
Dash black pepper	1 **teaspoon curry powder**
1½ **cups plain croutons**	¾ **teaspoon poultry seasoning**
1 **green apple, chopped**	⅛ **teaspoon garlic powder**

1. Preheat oven to 350°F. Lightly coat 2-quart baking dish with nonstick cooking spray.

2. Arrange chicken in single layer in prepared baking dish. Combine ¼ cup apple juice, salt and pepper in small bowl. Brush juice mixture over chicken.

3. Combine croutons, apple, onion, raisins, brown sugar, curry powder, seasoning and garlic powder in large bowl. Toss with remaining ¾ cup apple juice.

4. Spoon crouton mixture over chicken. Cover with foil; bake 45 minutes or until chicken is no longer pink in center.

Roast Turkey Breast with Sausage and Apple Stuffing

MAKES 6 SERVINGS

8 ounces bulk pork sausage

1 medium apple, peeled and finely chopped

1 shallot or small onion, finely chopped

1 stalk celery, finely chopped

¼ cup chopped hazelnuts

½ teaspoon rubbed sage, divided

½ teaspoon salt, divided

½ teaspoon black pepper, divided

1 tablespoon butter, softened

1 whole boneless turkey breast (4½ to 5 pounds), thawed if frozen

4 to 6 fresh sage leaves (optional)

1 cup chicken broth

1. Preheat oven to 325°F. Crumble sausage into large skillet. Add apple, shallot and celery; cook and stir over medium-high heat until sausage is cooked through and apple and vegetables are tender. Drain fat.

2. Stir in hazelnuts, ¼ teaspoon each rubbed sage, salt and pepper. Spoon mixture into shallow roasting pan.

3. Combine butter and remaining ¼ teaspoon each rubbed sage, salt and pepper. Spread over turkey breast. Arrange fresh sage leaves under skin, if desired. Place rack on top of stuffing. Place turkey, skin side down, on rack. Pour broth into pan.

4. Roast 45 minutes. Remove from oven; turn turkey skin side up. Baste with broth. Roast 1 hour or until meat thermometer registers 165°F. Let stand 10 minutes before slicing.

Chicken Apple Salad

¼ **cup mayonnaise**

2 **tablespoons sour cream**

1 **canned chipotle pepper in adobo sauce, minced**

½ **teaspoon ground cumin**

¼ **teaspoon salt**

¼ **teaspoon black pepper**

2 **cups chopped cooked chicken breast**

1 **cup diced unpeeled red or green apple**

½ **cup chopped red bell pepper or chopped roasted red peppers**

½ **cup diced celery**

⅓ **cup raisins**

⅓ **cup diced red onion**

1½ **ounces pecan pieces, toasted***

*To toast pecans, spread in single layer in heavy skillet. Cook and stir over medium heat 1 to 2 minutes or until nuts are lightly browned.

1. Stir mayonnaise, sour cream, chipotle pepper, cumin, salt and black pepper in medium bowl until smooth and well blended.

2. Add chicken, apple, bell pepper, celery, raisins and red onion; toss to coat. Stir in pecans just before serving.

Apple-Kissed Turkey Burgers

MAKES 4 SERVINGS

Butter-flavored vegetable cooking spray

¾ **pound ground turkey**

½ **cup chopped peeled apple**

2 **green onions, chopped (about ¼ cup)**

¾ **teaspoon lemon pepper**

¼ **teaspoon salt**

⅛ **teaspoon apple pie spice _or_ 1 pinch _each_ ground cinnamon and allspice**

½ **cup chili sauce**

½ **cup apple jelly**

4 **PEPPERIDGE FARM® Hamburger Rolls, split and toasted**

1. Heat the broiler. Spray a broiler pan with the cooking spray.

2. Thoroughly mix the turkey, apple, green onions, lemon pepper, salt and apple pie spice in a medium bowl. Shape the turkey mixture into **4** (¾-inch-thick) burgers.

3. Broil the burgers 6 inches from the heat for 10 minutes or until cooked through, turning them over once halfway through the broiling time.

4. Heat the chili sauce and jelly in a 1-quart saucepan over medium heat until the mixture is hot and bubbling, stirring occasionally.

5. Top the burgers with the chili sauce mixture. Serve the burgers on the rolls.

MAKE-AHEAD TIP: The turkey mixture and chili sauce mixture can be prepared a day in advance and refrigerated, tightly covered. Broil the burgers and reheat the sauce just before serving.

Apple 'n Cheddar Tuna Pitas

MAKES 4 SERVINGS

- **2 cans (5 ounces each) tuna in water, drained and flaked**
- **⅓ cup HELLMANN'S® or BEST FOODS® Real Mayonnaise**
- **¼ cup finely chopped celery**
- **¼ cup diced apple**
- **¼ cup dried cranberries**
- **¼ cup coarsely chopped walnuts (optional)**
- **4 slices Cheddar or American Cheese, cut up**
- **2 tablespoons finely chopped red onion (optional)**
- **2 (8-inch) plain or whole wheat pita breads, halved**

Combine all ingredients except pita breads in medium bowl. Evenly stuff pita breads with tuna mixture.

SUBSTITUTION: Also terrific with HELLMANN'S® or BEST FOODS® Light Mayonnaise or Mayonnaise Dressing with Olive Oil.

Wild Rice, Cranberry and Apple Stuffing

MAKES 8 SERVINGS

4 medium acorn squash (about 2¼ pounds)	**1 clove garlic, minced**
1 cup water	**1 cup hot cooked white or brown rice**
1 tablespoon olive oil or butter	**1 cup hot cooked wild rice**
1 medium apple, diced (about 1 cup)	**½ cup orange juice**
2 stalks diced celery (about ⅔ cup)	**¼ cup dried cranberries**
	¼ cup sliced green onions

1. Preheat oven to 400°F. Cut squash into halves. Scoop out and discard seeds. Place squash, cut sides down, in 13×9-inch baking dish. Add water to baking dish; bake 35 to 45 minutes or until fork-tender. Turn squash cut side up.

2. Heat oil in large saucepan over medium-high heat. Add apple, celery and garlic; cook and stir 5 minutes or until softened.

3. Reduce heat to medium-low. Add white rice, wild rice, orange juice and cranberries; cook 1 minute or until heated through.

4. Spoon rice mixture evenly into squash halves. Top evenly with green onions.

SERVING SUGGESTION: Serve alongside roast turkey, chicken or pork.

Side Dishes

Apple-Walnut Salad with Blue Cheese-Honey Vinaigrette

MAKES 4 SERVINGS

¼ **cup chopped walnuts**

1 **tablespoon white wine vinegar**

2 **teaspoons olive oil**

2 **teaspoons honey**

¼ **teaspoon salt**

⅛ **teaspoon black pepper**

2 **tablespoons crumbled blue cheese**

1 **large head Bibb lettuce, separated into leaves**

1 **small Red Delicious or other red apple, thinly sliced**

1 **small Granny Smith apple, thinly sliced**

1. Place walnuts in small skillet over medium heat. Cook and stir 5 minutes or until fragrant and lightly toasted. Transfer to plate to cool.

2. Whisk vinegar, oil, honey, salt and pepper in small bowl until well blended. Stir in cheese.

3. Divide lettuce and apples evenly among four plates. Drizzle dressing evenly over each salad; top with walnuts.

Apple-Cranberry Kugel

MAKES 6 SERVINGS

8 ounces uncooked extra-wide egg noodles

6 egg yolks

¾ cup sugar

1⅓ cups milk

1⅓ cups whipping cream

1 teaspoon vanilla

¼ teaspoon ground cinnamon

2 cups sliced apples

1 cup dried cranberries

1. Preheat oven to 350°F. Lightly coat 8-inch square baking dish with nonstick cooking spray. Cook noodles according to package directions; drain. Rinse under cold water; drain well.

2. Whisk egg yolks and sugar in large bowl until thick and pale yellow. Whisk in milk, cream, vanilla and cinnamon.

3. Toss noodles, apples and cranberries in separate large bowl until combined. Transfer to prepared baking dish. Pour 3 cups egg mixture over noodles. Cover casserole with foil. Bake 55 minutes or just until set. (The middle will set as it cools.)

4. Cook and stir remaining egg mixture in small saucepan over low heat 8 minutes or until mixture coats back of spoon. Drizzle over kugel.

Gingered Apple Cranberry Chutney

MAKES ABOUT 6 SERVINGS

- **2 medium Granny Smith apples, peeled and diced**
- **1 package (12 ounces) fresh or thawed frozen cranberries**
- **1¼ cups packed light brown sugar**
- **¾ cup cranberry juice cocktail**
- **½ cup golden raisins**
- **¼ cup chopped crystallized ginger**
- **¼ cup cider vinegar**
- **1 teaspoon ground cinnamon**
- **⅛ teaspoon ground allspice**

1. Combine apples, cranberries, brown sugar, cranberry juice cocktail, raisins, ginger, cider vinegar, cinnamon and allspice in heavy medium saucepan. Bring to a boil over high heat. Reduce heat to medium. Simmer 20 to 25 minutes or until mixture is very thick, stirring occasionally with wooden spoon.

2. Remove saucepan from heat. Cool completely. Store in airtight container in refrigerator up to 2 weeks.

Tip: You can enjoy Granny Smith apples year-round. After the fall American-grown crop is consumed, the harvest from New Zealand and Australia arrives in spring.

Tangy Rice, Apple and Cabbage Slaw

MAKES 6 TO 8 SERVINGS

⅔ cup Celery Seed Vinaigrette (recipe follows)

2 cups water

2 teaspoons butter

¼ teaspoon salt

¾ cup uncooked long grain rice

2 cups shredded red and green cabbage or prepared coleslaw mix

1½ cups chopped unpeeled tart red apples

½ cup chopped green onions

½ cup grated carrots

½ cup slivered almonds

1. Prepare Celery Seed Vinaigrette; set aside.

2. Bring water, butter and salt to a boil in medium saucepan over medium-high heat. Stir in rice. Reduce heat to low; simmer, covered, 20 minutes. Remove from heat. Let stand 5 minutes or until water is absorbed.

3. Combine cabbage, apples, green onions, carrots and almonds in large bowl. Add rice; mix well.

4. Stir in Celery Seed Vinaigrette; toss until well combined. Cover; refrigerate until ready to serve.

Celery Seed Vinaigrette

MAKES ¾ CUP

½ cup vegetable oil

3 tablespoons honey

2 tablespoons white wine vinegar

1 teaspoon celery seed

¾ teaspoon dry mustard

Salt

Combine oil, honey, vinegar, celery seed and mustard in small bowl; whisk until well blended. Season with salt.

Note: Celery Seed Vinaigrette can be prepared up to 2 days ahead. Cover and store in refrigerator. Whisk before using.

Baked Apple Cranberry Stuffing

MAKES 8 TO 10 SERVINGS

REYNOLDS WRAP® Non-Stick Foil

3 **tablespoons butter or margarine**

2 **cups sliced celery**

1 **cup chopped onion**

1 **bag (14 ounces) cubed herb-seasoned stuffing**

1 **medium Granny Smith apple, chopped**

1 **cup dried sweetened cranberries**

2¼ **cups chicken broth**

PREHEAT oven to 350°F. Line a 13×9×2-inch baking pan with REYNOLDS WRAP® Foil Non-Stick Foil with non-stick (dull) side toward food; set aside.

MELT butter in saucepan. Add celery and onion; cook until tender or place butter in a microwave-safe dish. Melt butter on HIGH, 1 to 2 minutes. Add celery and onion. Microwave on HIGH until tender, 5 to 8 minutes; set aside.

COMBINE stuffing, apple, dried cranberries and celery mixture in a large bowl. Gradually add broth to stuffing mixture, tossing until moistened. Spoon stuffing into foil-lined pan.

BAKE 35 to 40 minutes or until brown on top.

Curried Honey Mustard & Apple Dip

MAKES 2 CUPS

1 **cup mayonnaise**

¾ **cup sour cream**

⅓ **cup peeled and finely chopped apple**

¼ **cup finely chopped red onion**

1 **envelope WISH-BONE® Honey Mustard Dressing & Seasoning Mix**

½ **teaspoon curry powder**

Combine all ingredients in medium bowl. Cover and refrigerate 30 minutes or until ready to serve. Serve with your favorite dippers.

Corn Bread Stuffing with Sausage and Apples

MAKES 8 TO 12 SERVINGS

1 package (16 ounces) honey corn bread mix, plus ingredients to prepare mix

2 cups cubed French bread

1½ pounds mild Italian sausage, casings removed

1 onion, finely chopped

1 green apple, peeled and diced

2 stalks celery, finely chopped

½ teaspoon salt

¼ teaspoon dried sage

¼ teaspoon dried rosemary

¼ teaspoon dried thyme

¼ teaspoon black pepper

3 cups chicken broth

2 tablespoons chopped fresh Italian parsley (optional)

SLOW COOKER DIRECTIONS

1. Prepare and bake corn bread mix according to package directions. When cool, cover with plastic wrap and set aside overnight.*

2. Preheat oven to 350°F. Cut corn bread into 1-inch cubes. Spread corn bread and French bread on baking sheet. Bake 20 minutes or until dry.

3. Spray slow cooker with nonstick cooking spray. Brown sausage in medium skillet over medium heat, stirring to break up meat. Drain any fat; transfer sausage to slow cooker.

4. Add onion, apple and celery to skillet; cook and stir 5 minutes or until softened. Stir in salt, sage, rosemary, thyme and pepper. Remove to slow cooker.

5. Add bread cubes; stir gently to combine. Pour broth over mixture. Cover; cook on HIGH 3 to 3½ hours or until liquid is absorbed. Garnish with parsley.

Or, purchase a prepared 8-inch square pan of corn bread. Proceed as directed.

Scalloped Apples & Onions

MAKES 6 SERVINGS

1 medium onion, thinly sliced

4 tablespoons butter, melted, divided

5 red or green apples, cored and thinly sliced

8 ounces (1½ cups) pasteurized process cheese, cut into small pieces, divided

2 cups FRENCH'S® French Fried Onions, divided

1. Preheat oven to 375°F. Sauté onion in *2 tablespoons* butter in medium skillet over medium-high heat 3 minutes or until tender. Add apples and sauté 5 minutes or until apples are tender.

2. Stir *1 cup* cheese, *1 cup* French Fried Onions and remaining melted butter into apple mixture. Transfer to greased 9-inch deep-dish pie plate.

3. Bake, uncovered, 20 minutes or until heated through. Top with remaining cheese and onions. Bake 5 minutes or until cheese is melted.

Tip: To save time and cleanup, apple mixture may be baked in a heatproof skillet if desired. Wrap skillet handle in heavy-duty foil.

Baby Lettuces with Green Apple, Walnuts and Dried Cranberries

MAKES 4 SERVINGS

2 teaspoons fresh lemon juice

½ cup vanilla or plain low-fat yogurt

¼ teaspoon curry powder

½ to 1 teaspoon sugar

2½ tablespoons extra-virgin olive oil

Salt and black pepper

1 package (5 ounces) DOLE® Baby Garden Blend or DOLE® Sassy Baby Blend or other DOLE® Salad variety

1 DOLE® Green Apple halved, cored and thinly sliced

½ cup walnuts, toasted and roughly chopped

⅓ cup dried sweetened cranberries

• Mix lemon juice, yogurt, curry powder and sugar in small bowl. Whisk in olive oil and season with salt and pepper.

• Combine salad blend, apple slices, walnuts and cranberries in large bowl. Add yogurt dressing; gently toss to coat.

Apple Salsa Fresca

MAKES 6 SERVINGS

1 **Red Delicious apple, cored, diced**

1 **Granny Smith apple, cored, diced**
   Juice of ½ lime

3 **tablespoons orange juice**

½ **red onion, diced**

2 **tablespoons ORTEGA® Fire-Roasted Diced Green Chiles, drained**

¼ **cup ORTEGA® Salsa, any variety**

1 **tablespoon REGINA® Red Wine Vinegar**

1 **tablespoon packed brown sugar**

1 **teaspoon dried oregano**

TOSS apples with lime juice and orange juice in medium bowl. Add onion and chiles; toss again. Add salsa, vinegar, brown sugar and oregano; mix well. Serve at room temperature, or cover and refrigerate up to 2 hours.

Note: This salsa goes especially well with pork dishes and makes a great topping for salads.

Tip: Dice the apples in very small pieces and serve with broken ORTEGA® Yellow Corn Taco Shells as a healthy dip.

Spiced Vanilla Applesauce

MAKES 6 CUPS

5   **pounds (about 10 medium) sweet apples (such as Fuji or Gala), peeled and cut into 1-inch pieces**

½   **cup water**

2   **teaspoons vanilla**

1   **teaspoon ground cinnamon**

¼   **teaspoon ground nutmeg**

¼   **teaspoon ground cloves**

SLOW COOKER DIRECTIONS

1. Combine apples, water, vanilla, cinnamon, nutmeg and cloves in slow cooker; stir to blend. Cover; cook on HIGH 3 to 4 hours or until apples are very tender.

2. Turn off heat. Mash mixture with potato masher to smooth out any large lumps. Let cool completely before serving.

Tip: Cinnamon can vary in flavor depending on where it is grown. Some of the world's sweetest and strongest comes from China and Vietnam. Like most spices, ground cinnamon will lose its strength over time, so if yours has been in the cabinet for a while, sniff or taste it before using to make sure it is still flavorful.

Crisp, Crunchy Apple Slaw

MAKES 8 SERVINGS

2　**medium Granny Smith apples, cut into matchsticks**

½　**teaspoon grated lemon peel**

2　**tablespoons lemon juice**

1　**tablespoon sugar**

¼　**cup chopped fresh mint**

Combine apples, lemon peel, lemon juice, sugar and mint in medium bowl; toss gently. Serve immediately.

Tips: May be prepared up to 4 hours in advance. When using both the juice and peel of a lemon, grate the peel first, then squeeze the juice. (1 lemon = 3 tablespoons juice and about 2 teaspoons grated peel.) Add mint just before serving.

Swedish Apple Pie

MAKES 1 (9-INCH) PIE

4 **Granny Smith apples, peeled, cored and sliced**

1 **cup plus 1 tablespoon sugar, divided**

1 **tablespoon ground cinnamon**

¾ **cup (1½ sticks) butter, melted**

1 **cup all-purpose flour**

1 **egg**

½ **cup chopped nuts**

1. Preheat oven to 350°F.

2. Spread apples in 9-inch deep-dish pie plate or 9-inch square baking dish. Combine 1 tablespoon sugar and cinnamon in small bowl; sprinkle over apples and drizzle with butter. Combine remaining 1 cup sugar, flour, egg and nuts in medium bowl. (Mixture will be thick.) Spread batter over apples.

3. Bake 50 to 55 minutes or until top is golden brown.

Pies, Tarts and Crisps

Maple Walnut Apple Crescent Cobbler

MAKES 8 SERVINGS

FILLING

- **6 Golden Delicious apples (2½ pounds), peeled and thinly sliced**
- **⅓ cup maple syrup**
- **2 tablespoons all-purpose flour**
- **2 teaspoons vanilla**
- **⅛ teaspoon ground nutmeg**

TOPPING

- **1 package (8 ounces) refrigerated crescent roll dough**
- **4 teaspoons butter, melted**
- **¼ cup chopped walnuts**
- **2 tablespoons packed brown sugar**

1. Preheat oven to 375°F. Spray 8-inch square baking dish with nonstick cooking spray.

2. Combine apples, syrup, flour, vanilla and nutmeg in medium bowl; toss to coat. Spoon into prepared baking dish. Bake 30 minutes or until apples are tender but still firm.

3. Meanwhile, divide crescent roll dough into eight triangles; place on work surface. Brush top of each triangle with melted butter. Combine walnuts and brown sugar in small bowl; sprinkle over dough. Roll up each dough triangle to form crescent. Arrange crescents over warm apple mixture in two rows.

4. Bake in center of oven 15 minutes. Cover loosely with foil; bake 30 minutes. Uncover; bake 3 minutes or until filling is thick and bubbly and crescent rolls are golden brown.

Apple-Pear Praline Pie

MAKES 8 SERVINGS

Double-Crust Pie Pastry (recipe follows)

4 cups sliced peeled Granny Smith apples

2 cups sliced peeled pears

¾ cup granulated sugar

¼ cup plus 1 tablespoon all-purpose flour, divided

4 teaspoons ground cinnamon

¼ teaspoon salt

½ cup (1 stick) plus 2 tablespoons butter, divided

1 cup packed brown sugar

1 tablespoon half-and-half or milk

1 cup chopped pecans

1. Prepare Double-Crust Pie Pastry.

2. Combine apples, pears, granulated sugar, ¼ cup flour, cinnamon and salt in large bowl; toss to coat. Let stand 15 minutes.

3. Preheat oven to 350°F. Roll out one disc of pastry into 11-inch circle on floured surface. Line deep-dish 9-inch pie plate with pastry; sprinkle with remaining 1 tablespoon flour. Spoon apple and pear mixture into crust; dot with 2 tablespoons butter. Roll out remaining disc of pastry into 10-inch circle. Place over fruit; seal and flute edge. Cut slits in top crust.

4. Bake 1 hour. Meanwhile, combine remaining ½ cup butter, brown sugar and half-and-half in small saucepan; bring to a boil over medium heat, stirring frequently. Boil 2 minutes, stirring constantly. Remove from heat; stir in pecans. Spread over pie.

5. Cool pie on wire rack 15 minutes. Serve warm or at room temperature.

DOUBLE-CRUST PIE PASTRY: Combine 2½ cups all-purpose flour, 1 teaspoon salt and 1 teaspoon sugar in large bowl. Cut in 1 cup (2 sticks) cubed unsalted butter with pastry blender or two knives until coarse crumbs form. Drizzle ⅓ cup water over flour mixture, 2 tablespoons at a time, stirring just until dough comes together. Divide dough in half. Form each half into disc; wrap in plastic wrap. Refrigerate 30 minutes.

Fresh Apple and Toffee Tart

MAKES 2 TARTS (8 SERVINGS EACH)

4 to 6 large tart apples such as Granny Smith

¼ cup granulated sugar

2 tablespoons cornstarch or all-purpose flour

½ teaspoon ground cinnamon

1 package (15-ounce box) refrigerated pie crusts, softened as directed on box

1⅓ cups (8-ounce package) HEATH® BITS 'O BRICKLE® Toffee Bits, divided

2 teaspoons white decorator sugar crystals or granulated sugar, divided

Sweetened whipped cream or ice cream (optional)

1. Heat oven to 400°F. Peel and slice apples into thin slices. Toss apples with granulated sugar, cornstarch and cinnamon.

2. Unroll crusts; place each on ungreased cookie sheet. Sprinkle ⅓ cup toffee bits over each crust; press lightly into crust.

3. Starting 2 inches from the edge of the crust, arrange apple slices by overlapping slightly in a circular spiral toward the center of the crust. Sprinkle ⅓ cup of remaining toffee bits over each apple center. Fold 2-inch edge of crust over apples. Sprinkle each crust edge with 1 teaspoon sugar crystals.

4. Bake 25 to 30 minutes or until crust is golden. Cool slightly. Serve warm or cool with sweetened whipped cream or ice cream, if desired.

Note: Recipe may be halved.

Crumble-Topped Apple Pie

MAKES 8 SERVINGS

2 cups all-purpose flour, divided

2 cups granulated sugar, divided

¼ teaspoon salt, divided

14 tablespoons I CAN'T BELIEVE IT'S NOT BUTTER® All Purpose Sticks, divided

1 to 2 tablespoons ice water

½ cup firmly packed brown sugar

½ cup quick-cooking oats

1 teaspoon ground cinnamon

4 medium apples, peeled, cored and thinly sliced

2 teaspoons fresh lemon juice

1. Preheat oven to 425°F. Preheat baking sheet.

2. For crust, combine 1 cup flour, 1½ cups granulated sugar and ⅛ teaspoon salt in medium bowl. Cut in 6 tablespoons I Can't Believe It's Not Butter!® All Purpose Sticks with pastry blender or two knives until coarse crumbs form. Add ice water, 1 tablespoon at a time, until dough forms. Knead dough with floured hands just until mixture forms a ball. Roll dough on lightly floured surface from center to edges to form a 12-inch circle. Press into 9-inch pie plate; set aside.

3. For crumb topping, combine ¾ cup flour, brown sugar, oats and cinnamon in medium bowl. Cut in remaining 8 tablespoons All Purpose Sticks with pastry blender or two knives to form large coarse crumbs; set aside.

4. Combine remaining ¼ cup flour, remaining ½ cup granulated sugar and remaining ⅛ teaspoon salt in small bowl; set aside.

5. Toss apples with lemon juice, then flour mixture in large bowl. Arrange apple mixture in pie crust. Evenly top with crumb mixture, pressing down gently. Arrange pie on heated baking sheet, then decrease oven to 375°F. Bake 1 hour 5 minutes or until juices are bubbling. Cool on wire rack.

6. Serve, if desired, with BREYERS® French Vanilla or Natural Vanilla Ice Cream.

Tip: If you're time-challenged, use a store-brought single crust pie shell.

Cran-Apple & Almond Tart

MAKES 12 SERVINGS

½ of a (17.3 ounce package) **PEPPERIDGE FARM®** Frozen Puff Pastry Sheets (1 sheet)

1 package (7 ounces) almond paste

5 tablespoons butter, softened

2 eggs

½ cup all-purpose flour

Water

⅓ cup dried cranberries

2 medium Golden Delicious apples, peeled and thinly sliced (about 3 cups)

1 tablespoon sugar

Sugar Glaze (recipe follows)

1. Thaw the pastry sheet at room temperature for 40 minutes or until it's easy to handle. Heat the oven to 400°F. Lightly grease a baking sheet.

2. Put the almond paste in a food processor. Cover and process until it's finely ground. Add the butter, eggs and flour. Cover and process until the mixture is smooth.

3. Unfold the pastry sheet on a lightly floured surface. Roll the sheet into a 14×10-inch rectangle. Place on the baking sheet. Brush the edges of the rectangle with water. Fold over the edges ½ inch on all sides, pressing firmly to form a rim. Prick the pastry thoroughly with a fork (do not prick the rim).

4. Spread the almond mixture evenly over the pastry. Top with cranberries. Arrange the apple slices on top. Sprinkle with the sugar.

5. Bake for 25 minutes or until golden and apples are tender. Make the Sugar Glaze 10 minutes before the tart is finished baking. Immediately brush the glaze over the tart. Cool completely on a wire rack.

SUGAR GLAZE: Put **½ cup** confectioners' sugar in a small bowl. Stir in **2 tablespoons** milk until smooth. Add a little more milk if the glaze is too thick.

Apple Blackberry Crisp

MAKES 6 SERVINGS

4 cups sliced peeled apples

Juice of ½ lemon

2 tablespoons granulated sugar

2 tablespoons Irish cream liqueur

1 teaspoon ground cinnamon, divided

1 cup old-fashioned oats

6 tablespoons (¾ stick) cold butter, cut into small pieces

⅔ cup packed brown sugar

¼ cup all-purpose flour

1 cup fresh blackberries

Irish Whipped Cream (recipe follows, optional)

1. Preheat oven to 375°F. Grease 9-inch oval or 8-inch square baking dish.

2. Place apples in large bowl; drizzle with lemon juice. Add granulated sugar, liqueur and ½ teaspoon cinnamon; toss to coat.

3. Combine oats, butter, brown sugar, flour and remaining ½ teaspoon cinnamon in food processor; pulse unti combined, leaving some some chunks remaining.

4. Gently stir blackberries into apple mixture. Spoon into prepared baking dish; sprinkle with oat mixture.

5. Bake 30 to 40 minutes or until filling is bubbly and topping is golden brown. Prepare Irish Whipped Cream, if desired; serve with crisp.

IRISH WHIPPED CREAM: Beat 1 cup whipping cream and 2 tablespoons Irish cream liqueur in large bowl with electric mixer at high speed until slightly thickened. Add 1 to 2 tablespoons powdered sugar; beat until soft peaks form.

Tip: This crisp can also be made without the blackberries; just add an additional 1 cup sliced apples.

Old-Fashioned Apple Pie

MAKES 8 TO 10 SERVINGS

REYNOLDS® Parchment Paper

Pastry for 9-inch deep dish, double crust pie, prepared

4 to 5 cups (3 pounds) tart cooking apples, peeled, cored and sliced

1¼ cups sugar

⅓ cup flour

1 teaspoon ground cinnamon

1 tablespoon butter

2 teaspoons milk

½ teaspoon sugar

PREHEAT oven to 350°F. Roll out half of pastry to ⅛-inch thickness on a sheet of REYNOLDS® Parchment Paper. Place in 9-inch deep dish pie plate; set aside. Combine apples, sugar, flour and cinnamon in a large bowl; mix to coat apples. Spoon mixture evenly into pie crust; top with butter.

ROLL remaining pastry for top crust to ⅛-inch thickness on a floured sheet of REYNOLDS® Parchment Paper. Place on top of pie. Trim off excess pastry along edges. Fold edges under and crimp. Cut design in center to allow steam to escape. Brush pastry lightly with milk; sprinkle with sugar.

BAKE 45 to 50 minutes or until crust is golden brown. Serve warm.

Apple Custard Pie

MAKES 8 SERVINGS

- ½ cup **KARO® Light or Dark Corn Syrup**
- ½ cup **sugar**
- ¼ cup **ARGO® or KINGSFORD'S® Corn Starch**
- 3 **eggs**
- ½ cup **margarine or butter, melted**
- 1 **teaspoon vanilla extract**
- 2 **large apples, peeled and thinly sliced**
- 1 **unbaked (9-inch) pie crust**
- 2 **tablespoons chopped walnuts (optional)**

In medium bowl, combine sugar and corn starch. Whisk in eggs. Stir in margarine, corn syrup and vanilla extract. Fold in half of the apples. Pour into pie crust.

Place remaining apples in overlapping circle on top of pie. Sprinkle with walnuts.

Bake in 375°F oven 50 minutes or until center of pie is set. Cool on wire rack.

Sour Cream Apple Tart

MAKES 12 SERVINGS

5 tablespoons butter, divided

¾ cup graham cracker crumbs

1¼ teaspoons ground cinnamon, divided

1⅓ cups sour cream

¾ cup sugar, divided

½ cup all-purpose flour, divided

2 eggs

1 teaspoon vanilla

5 cups coarsely chopped peeled Jonathan apples or other firm red-skinned apples

1. Preheat oven to 350°F.

2. Melt 3 tablespoons butter in small saucepan over medium heat. Stir in graham cracker crumbs and ¼ teaspoon cinnamon until well blended. Press crumb mixture firmly onto bottom of 9-inch springform pan. Bake 10 minutes. Remove to wire rack to cool.

3. Beat sour cream, ½ cup sugar and 2 tablespoons plus 1½ teaspoons flour in large bowl with electric mixer at medium speed until well blended. Beat in eggs and vanilla until well blended. Stir in apples. Spoon into prepared crust.

4. Bake 35 minutes or just until center is set. Cut into 12 slices.

5. Preheat broiler. Combine remaining 1 teaspoon cinnamon, ¼ cup sugar and 5 tablespoons plus 1½ teaspoons flour in small bowl. Cut in remaining 2 tablespoons butter with pastry blender until mixture resembles coarse crumbs. Sprinkle over top of pie.

6. Broil 3 to 4 minutes or until topping is golden brown. Let stand 15 minutes before serving.

Apple-Pomegranate Crisp

MAKES 8 SERVINGS

SYRUP

- **1 cup pomegranate juice**
- **¼ cup sugar**
- **1 teaspoon cornstarch**
- **1 teaspoon ground cinnamon**

FILLING

- **4 medium Granny Smith apples, thinly sliced**
- **⅓ cup CREAM OF WHEAT® Apples 'n Cinnamon Instant Hot Cereal, uncooked, divided**

- **1 cup pomegranate arils**

TOPPING

- **½ cup all-purpose flour**
- **¼ cup sugar**
- **1 teaspoon ground cinnamon**
- **¼ teaspoon salt**
- **2 tablespoons cold butter, cut into ½-inch pieces**
- **2 tablespoons apple juice**
- **Frozen low-fat yogurt (optional)**

1. Preheat oven to 350°F. Whisk pomegranate juice, sugar, cornstarch and cinnamon in medium saucepan until well blended. Bring to a boil over medium heat. Cook 5 minutes or until thickened, stirring constantly. Remove syrup from heat; set aside.

2. Toss apples with ¼ cup Cream of Wheat. Divide evenly among 8 (6-ounce) ramekins or ovenproof bowls. Top evenly with pomegranate arils and prepared syrup; set aside.

3. Combine flour, sugar, cinnamon, salt and remaining Cream of Wheat in medium bowl. Cut in butter with pastry blender until mixture resembles coarse crumbs. Stir in apple juice until well blended. Sprinkle topping evenly over apple mixture in each ramekin.

4. Bake 25 to 30 minutes or until apples are tender and topping is golden brown. Serve warm. Top with frozen yogurt, if desired.

Tip: Arils are the juicy ruby-red sacs inside fresh pomegranates that contain a tiny edible seed. To extract them from the pomegranate with no mess, section the pomegranate, and place the sections in a bowl of water. Separate the arils from the inedible membrane, and discard the skin and membrane. Lift the arils from the water and drain well before using.

Apple-Cranberry Tart

MAKES 8 SERVINGS

1⅓ cups all-purpose flour

¾ cup plus 1 tablespoon sugar, divided

¼ teaspoon salt

2 tablespoons shortening

2 tablespoons margarine

4 to 5 tablespoons ice water

½ cup boiling water

⅓ cup dried cranberries

1 teaspoon ground cinnamon

2 tablespoons cornstarch

4 medium baking apples

Vanilla frozen yogurt (optional)

1. Combine flour, 1 tablespoon sugar and salt in medium bowl. Cut in shortening and margarine with pastry blender or two knives until mixture forms coarse crumbs. Mix in ice water, 1 tablespoon at a time, until mixture comes together and forms soft dough. Wrap in plastic wrap. Refrigerate 30 minutes.

2. Combine boiling water and cranberries in small bowl. Let stand 20 minutes or until softened.

3. Preheat oven to 425°F. Roll out dough on floured surface to ⅛-inch thickness. Cut into 11-inch circle. (Reserve any leftover dough scraps for decorating top of tart.) Ease dough into 10-inch tart pan with removable bottom, leaving ¼-inch dough above rim of pan. Prick bottom and sides of dough with tines of fork; bake 12 minutes or until dough begins to brown. Cool on wire rack. *Reduce oven temperature to 375°F.*

4. Combine remaining ¾ cup sugar and cinnamon in large bowl; mix well. Reserve 1 teaspoon mixture. Add cornstarch to bowl. Peel, core and thinly slice apples, adding pieces after sliced; toss well. Drain cranberries; add to apple mixture and toss well.

5. Arrange apple mixture attractively over dough. Sprinkle reserved 1 teaspoon sugar mixture evenly over top of tart. Place tart on baking sheet; bake 30 to 35 minutes or until apples are tender and crust is golden brown. Cool on wire rack. Remove side of pan; place tart on serving plate. Serve warm or at room temperature with frozen yogurt, if desired.

Acknowledgments

The publisher would like to thank the companies and organizations listed below for the use of their recipes and photographs in this publication.

ACH Food Companies, Inc.

The Beef Checkoff

Cabot® Creamery Cooperative

Campbell Soup Company

The Coca-Cola Company®

Cream of Wheat® Cereal, A Division of B&G Foods North America, Inc.

Dole Food Company, Inc.

Heinz North America

The Hershey Company

jarlsbergusa.com

Ortega®, A Division of B&G Foods North America, Inc.

Pinnacle Foods

Reckitt Benckiser LLC

Recipes courtesy of the Reynolds Kitchens

Unilever

CINNAMON CHIP
APPLESAUCE
COFFEE CAKE
P. 4

Index

Metric Conversion Chart

VOLUME MEASUREMENTS (dry)

⅛ teaspoon = 0.5 mL
¼ teaspoon = 1 mL
½ teaspoon = 2 mL
¾ teaspoon = 4 mL
1 teaspoon = 5 mL
1 tablespoon = 15 mL
2 tablespoons = 30 mL
¼ cup = 60 mL
⅓ cup = 75 mL
½ cup = 125 mL
⅔ cup = 150 mL
¾ cup = 175 mL
1 cup = 250 mL
2 cups = 1 pint = 500 mL
3 cups = 750 mL
4 cups = 1 quart = 1 L

VOLUME MEASUREMENTS (fluid)

1 fluid ounce (2 tablespoons) = 30 mL
4 fluid ounces (½ cup) = 125 mL
8 fluid ounces (1 cup) = 250 mL
12 fluid ounces (1½ cups) = 375 mL
16 fluid ounces (2 cups) = 500 mL

WEIGHTS (mass)

½ ounce = 15 g
1 ounce = 30 g
3 ounces = 90 g
4 ounces = 120 g
8 ounces = 225 g
10 ounces = 285 g
12 ounces = 360 g
16 ounces = 1 pound = 450 g

DIMENSIONS

1/16 inch = 2 mm
⅛ inch = 3 mm
¼ inch = 6 mm
½ inch = 1.5 cm
¾ inch = 2 cm
1 inch = 2.5 cm

OVEN TEMPERATURES

250°F = 120°C
275°F = 140°C
300°F = 150°C
325°F = 160°C
350°F = 180°C
375°F = 190°C
400°F = 200°C
425°F = 220°C
450°F = 230°C

BAKING PAN SIZES

Utensil	Size in Inches/Quarts	Metric Volume	Size in Centimeters
Baking or Cake Pan (square or rectangular)	8×8×2	2 L	20×20×5
	9×9×2	2.5 L	23×23×5
	12×8×2	3 L	30×20×5
	13×9×2	3.5 L	33×23×5
Loaf Pan	8×4×3	1.5 L	20×10×7
	9×5×3	2 L	23×13×7
Round Layer Cake Pan	8×1½	1.2 L	20×4
	9×1½	1.5 L	23×4
Pie Plate	8×1¼	750 mL	20×3
	9×1¼	1 L	23×3
Baking Dish or Casserole	1 quart	1 L	—
	1½ quart	1.5 L	—
	2 quart	2 L	—